I
Hear
His
Whisper

52
DEVOTIONS

BRIAN SIMMONS

BroadStreet
PUBLISHING

I Hear His Whisper
52 Devotions to Encounter God's Heart for You

Copyright © 2015 Brian Simmons

Published by BroadStreet Publishing Group, LLC
Racine, Wisconsin, USA
www.broadstreetpublishing.com

ISBN-13: 978-1-4245-4987-0 (hard cover)
ISBN-13: 978-1-4245-5015-9 (e-book)

All Scripture is from *The Passion Translation*® (*The Psalms: Poetry on Fire*; *Proverbs: Wisdom from Above*; *Song of Songs: Divine Romance*; *Luke and Acts: To the Lovers of God*; *John: Eternal Love*; *Letters from Heaven: By the Apostle Paul*; *Hebrews and James: Faith Works*; and *Job*. Copyright © 2014. Used by permission of BroadStreet Publishing Group, LLC, Racine, Wisconsin, USA. All rights reserved. www.thepassiontranslation.com.

Design by Garborg Design Works, Inc. | www.garborgdesign.com
Interior typesetting by Katherine Lloyd | www.theDESKonline.com

Printed in China

16 17 18 19 20   7 6 5 4 3

Introduction

I love to be alone with Jesus in the early morning hours. Many mornings before the sun is up I have spent time to hear and listen to the voice I have come to love. God whispers to those who seek Him. Yes, He will thunder with a mighty sound, but He will also whisper His words of love into our hearts.

This is the first compilation of the messages of love I have heard spoken into my heart. While God has spoken these words to me personally, each whisper will also have application for your life. For example, God welcomes each of us to know that "I am enough," and respond to His invitation to "Give your heart to Me."

God is not silent. He has a voice, and you can learn to hear it for yourself. I trust these "whispers" will spark in you the desire to hear God's gentle voice for yourself.

These words are not meant to replace God's eternal, inspired Word. The Bible speaks clearly and gives us truth unfiltered. I suggest you have your Bible close at hand as your read through these pages. Search the Scriptures to ensure what I present agrees with God's Word. God loves His people and longs for them to know Him, to hear His voice, and to obey His Word.

If you enjoy these whispers and don't want to wait for the next volume in this format, I regularly share other whispers at www.facebook.com/passiontranslation.

May the God of love bring you into His "cloud-filled chamber" as He whispers His eternal truths to you!

—Brian Simmons

For your whispers
in the night give me wisdom,
showing me what to do next.

Psalm 16:7 TPT

I hear His whisper...

"Come and rest with Me."

I care deeply for you, My child. There is nothing that you feel or experience that I don't also experience as I carry you through life. My hand is upon you, and nothing will take you away from My love. Quietly wait on Me, and you will feel my nearness. You will hear Me whisper into your soul, and My peace will descend upon you.

My little one, there is a hiding place you can find in Me. The shadow you see over you is the shadow of My wings. It is not a shadow of confusion, but a shadow of My hiding place where I will place you next to My heart. For I have taken you from troubled waters and brought you up on high to rest in My presence. No matter how dark the night and how fierce the trial, My kiss of mercy will keep and protect you.

No one says in My presence, "I am afraid." It is never heard in My glory, "I am poor." For I have given you all things that will strengthen your life and prepare you for eternity. In My presence all cry, "Glory." Come into the shelter of My shadow, where all My lovers are washed, robed, crowned, and seated with Me. I care deeply for you, and nothing can disturb you in the hiding place of My glory. Come and rest with Me.

PSALM 91:1–4

When you sit enthroned under the shadow of Shaddai,
* you are hidden in the strength of God Most High.*
He's the hope that holds me, and the Stronghold to shelter me,
* the only God for me, and my great Confidence.*
He will rescue you from every hidden trap of the enemy,
* and he will protect you from false accusation*
* and any deadly curse.*
His massive arms are wrapped around you, protecting you.
* You can run under his covering of majesty and hide.*
* His arms of faithfulness are a shield keeping you from harm.*

Is your soul troubled today? Take a moment to envision yourself under the shield of His arms or in the shadow of His wings. How does His shelter feel over you?

_____

_____

_____

_____

_____

_____

_____

_____

_____

_____

_____

_____

_____

_____

_____

_____

_____

"I am enough."

I am enough for you. When you face difficulties and limitations, I will whisper into your heart, "I am enough." I will not shield you from every hardship, but I am enough as you walk through them with your eyes set on Me. I am enough. I will be your wraparound shield in the midst of your difficulty.

When you are lonely and seek companionship, I am enough. When your heart is troubled over many things, you must bring your soul before Me, for I am enough. When the lies men have spoken bring disturbance into your mind, I will wash them away, for My Word is enough.

Your thoughts cannot contain the love I have for you. And you will never be able to comprehend with your mind the plans that I have for you. Yet I am enough, and all you need to know is that I am here for you.

My Spirit longs to satisfy every part of you: your mind, your soul, your desires, your longings. When darkness comes, I am enough to see you through the night. Many have found that, even in the deepest pain, I am still enough. Come and learn the secrets of satisfying grace.

I am about to bring you into a place where you have never been before. A place of contentment and peace that the world cannot impart. You will see how I have prepared you all your life for this day of destiny. The coming season will be extraordinary and filled with delight. Answers to your prayers that were prayed long ago will be soon in coming. What looked like delay after delay will make sense to you as the clouds part and the light of glory shines through.

You must know, My child, that I am enough. I am greater than your dreams, greater than your plans, and greater than your thoughts could ever be. Come and learn the secret that all My lovers learn: I am enough for you.

JOHN 14:5–7

Thomas said to him, "Master, we don't know where you're going, so how could we know the way there?" Jesus explained, "I am the Way, I am the Truth, and I am the Life. No one comes next to the Father except through union with me. To know me is to know my Father too. And from now on you will realize that you have seen him and experienced him."

Reflect on the idea that He is enough. In what areas of your life do you especially need to hear Him whisper this today? List them out and allow His satisfying grace to cover them.

_____

_____

_____

_____

_____

_____

_____

_____

_____

_____

_____

_____

_____

_____

_____

_____

_____

_____

_____

"Joy will get you through!"

The time of unhindered joy is here. I am exposing the treachery of the enemy. He has come more than once to your door to entice you away from the joy of the Lord. Accusations have come, bad news has been proclaimed, disappointment has tried to enter your family, but I say to you: My joy will get you through. No longer will you allow discouragement to win the day, for I am the God of joyous breakthrough! Have you not found gladness as you have served Me and prayed to Me? This is only a foretaste of the bliss I have reserved and stored up for you. The future will be nothing like your past, so leap for joy, shout for joy, and dance with joy!

Have no fear of anything, for nothing can take from you the presence of My Spirit. Joy is your portion, your inheritance, and the fruit of My Spirit. Taste the delicious fruit of joy, and sweetness will enter your inner being. The ecstasy of knowing Me must triumph in this hour.

Did I not say to My disciples in the midst of their storm, "Be of good cheer. It is I, be not afraid"? These are the same words I say to you today. Sing for joy. Do all that I have called you to do with sacred delight, for I bless you beyond measure, more than hundredfold. Let your joyous laughter be heard in your home, and watch what I will do to change your environment. Hold nothing back, for the enemy is threatened when you taste of My joy and enter into My gladness. Rejoice, and rejoice, and rejoice! Joy will get you through into the new place I'm calling you to. Today is the day made for you, so rejoice and be filled with gladness, for I am your God!

PSALM 100:4–5

Come right into his presence with thanksgiving.
  Come bring your thank-offering to him
  and affectionately bless his beautiful name!
For the Lord is always good and ready to receive you.
  He's so loving that it will amaze you—
  so kind that it will astound you!
  And he is famous for his faithfulness toward all.
  Everyone knows our God can be trusted,
  for he keeps his promises to every generation!

List the ways God has kept His promises to you and your family. Then express your gratitude to Him extravagantly. Proclaim that "he is famous for his faithfulness toward all"!

_____

_____

_____

_____

_____

_____

_____

_____

_____

_____

_____

_____

_____

_____

_____

_____

_____

I hear His whisper...

"I know you."

Many times you have thought that no one understands. People have walked away from you and have broken the bonds of friendship. But I know you. I know everything there is to know about you, and I will never walk away. My love is as constant as the light of the sun. It may seem dimmed at times, but in the breaking of a new day, My love burns brightly upon you.

You cannot hide your weaknesses from me. I have searched your soul and I know you. I discern every movement of your heart and I know the things you will speak before you have even formed a sentence. The thoughts of your heart live before Me and are completely open to Me. My eyes are washed in love and My hand is a hand of tenderness. When others speak evil, I whisper: "I know you and I love you."

Nothing takes Me by surprise, for I have filled all of time and eternity with My glory. I know your normal, everyday movements—when you sit and when you stand, when you are discouraged and when you laugh. I have charted the path ahead for you. I know every step you will take before your journey even begins. I am acquainted with all of your ways because I have known you before you were even born. I have chosen you to be My friend, My lover, My child.

There is no one on earth who understands you as I do—your motives, your dreams, your hopes, and your innermost longings. Come to be with the One who knows all there is to know and cherishes you for eternity. A deep understanding of My love will heal and strengthen you for all that is ahead. You have Me as a Perfect Father and I give only what is good to the children of light. I know you, My child, and My changeless love will fill your days with unending delight.

PSALM 139:1–4

Lord, you know everything there is to know about me.
  You've examined my innermost being with your loving gaze.
You perceive every movement of my heart and soul
  and understand my every thought before it even enters my mind.
You are so intimately aware of me, Lord.
  You read my heart like an open book
  and you know all the words I'm about to speak
  before I even start a sentence!
  You know every step I will take before my journey even begins!

What are you glad God knows about you—good things that others may not see or misunderstand? Thank Him for His changeless love and that He sees you with His loving gaze.

_____

_____

_____

_____

_____

_____

_____

_____

_____

_____

_____

_____

_____

_____

_____

_____

"Move forward."

The time has come for you to advance. You have remained in the place you are for long enough. You have crossed over a bridge and found the pleasant path that leads deeper into My heart. Move forward, My child.

As I promised Joshua, I promise you—every place that you set your foot upon will be yours. New territory is waiting. A calling pulls you onward. Move forward, My child, and you will see the works of your God. Faith never remains in one place; it is a movement, a dynamo that propels you forward. Nothing can stop you when I am with you and I call you forward.

The fullness of My plan is ahead of you. The sweet taste of joy has filled your heart, but there is more for you as you leave the predictable and move forward, My child. It is waiting for you. Step into all that I have chosen to bring to pass in your life.

Faith will not hesitate when My cloud has moved. I will direct you with My cloud and with My presence. Never be afraid to step out, and you will find more of Me. I have gone before you to prepare the way, and I will be your peace. I delight in you and will never leave you, for you are Mine.

PHILIPPIANS 3:12–14

I run with passion into his abundance so that I may reach the destiny that Jesus Christ has called me to fulfill and wants me to discover. I don't depend on my own strength to accomplish this; however I do have one compelling focus: I forget all of the past as I fasten my heart to the future instead. I run straight for the divine invitation of reaching the heavenly goal and gaining the victory-prize through the anointing of Jesus.

Where is He calling you to move forward today?
Write a declaration of faith and believe that He will
meet you as you step out into new territory.

_____

_____

_____

_____

_____

_____

_____

_____

_____

_____

_____

_____

_____

_____

_____

_____

_____

_____

"Live in My Spirit."

I am calling you to leave behind the reasoning of this world, the opinions and traditions of men, and come into true life with Me. You have lived in your mind; now live in My Spirit. The realm of the Holy Spirit is opened by My grace so that you can know me not in your mind but with your spirit. My Spirit will give to you gifts, fruit, wisdom, and power. Live in My Spirit, and you will find your true destiny.

The table of fellowship has been prepared. Come and dine with Me and enter into a greater joy, the joy of communion of the Holy Spirit. The highest joys and the best path for you will be found by living in My Spirit.

Feed your spirit with My Life, and you will be transformed from the inside out. The new reality I am calling you to is the reality of life in Me. The ways of man cannot bring you the joys of heaven.

If you ask Me, I will come and bring you deeper understanding of My ways. If you ask Me for life, I will not bring you confusion. If you ask Me for living bread, I will not give you anything less than My best.

You can trust Me, so ask, and you will receive the fullness of My Spirit. Live in My Spirit, and you will discover who I have made you to be.

LUKE 11:11–13

"Do you know of any father who would give his son a snake on a plate when he asked for a serving of fish? Of course not! Do you know of any father who would give his daughter a spider when she had asked for an egg? Of course not! If imperfect parents know how to lovingly take care of their children and give them what they need, how much more will the perfect heavenly Father give the Holy Spirit's fullness when his children ask him."

When have you experienced the fullness of His Spirit in the past? In what areas do you need Him to fill you today? Write a few examples of each, and allow the joy of His past filling to boost your appetite for His Spirit today.

_____

_____

_____

_____

_____

_____

_____

_____

_____

_____

_____

_____

_____

_____

_____

_____

I hear His whisper…

"Hold on to Me!"

In your days of trouble and your days of glory, in your days of testing and your days of triumph—hold on to Me! The changes will now come more swiftly than you have imagined. That which looms before you may challenge your faith, but hold on to Me!

Your help comes from Me and from nowhere else. Many look to others to be there for them, but I say to you, I will always be there for you. Trust in Me. Let your challenges bring you to a greater faith, for My outstretched arm of power will bring you courage—hold on to Me!

Those who trust in Me see miracles. In these days of intense struggle, when it looks like darkness is winning and your light is growing dim, hold on to Me!

I have taught you many things. You have learned that walking with Me is more valuable and pleasing than your comforts. You have sacrificed your plans for Mine, and you have given Me the reins of your heart. I am satisfied with your tender surrender. You have trusted My ways even when they were nothing but a mystery to you. Many times you bowed your heart in worship. These are the times you grew in grace and took giant leaps of faith. Keep moving into My heart even as things shift all around you. Hold on to Me, and you will have all that you have ever desired, for I am pleased to be your Father and your God.

PSALM 72:5

The sun and moon will stop shining
  before your lovers will stop worshipping;
  for ages upon ages the people will love and adore you!

Is this a week of trial or triumph?
Write a prayer confessing your need for His courage
or expressing your thankfulness for His help.

_____

_____

_____

_____

_____

_____

_____

_____

_____

_____

_____

_____

_____

_____

_____

_____

_____

_____

"Don't strive."

I have taught you in the secret place and you have learned the ways of My Spirit. I remind you this day: do not strive, but rest your heart in the quietness and I will do what you cannot do. Anxiety and striving are the worst of enemies to your peace. When I give you a task, I give you the grace to accomplish it. I will never send you to fail or give you a mission only to make you fall. I will strengthen you in the quiet place and bring My transcendent presence to calm your soul.

Many of my children are trying to correct the path of another, not knowing that I am at work in them, even as I am at work in you. Rest in my love and I will bring it to pass, and I will bring you transformation by the renewing of your mind. Let Me bring you into a greater light with greater insight. You will begin to see what I am doing in the life of another and pray for them with divine wisdom. Until you come higher into My light, you will misunderstand all that I am doing.

When you know Me, you will no longer strive to be better or strive to be loved. When you experience My endless compassion, you will learn to forgive. To strive is to leave My strength and embrace the cares of life. To refuse to strive means you will enter into the faith-rest life that I give to all those who love Me. Faith rests in hope. Know that I will never fail you or disappoint you. So My child, this is the day of Sabbath joy when you will enter into the realm of My kingdom.

HEBREWS 4:3

For those of us who believe, faith activates the promise and we experience the realm of confident rest!

In what way have you been striving lately? Have you found yourself striving to correct someone else's path? Write a prayer releasing these cares into His hands.

_____
_____
_____
_____
_____
_____
_____
_____
_____
_____
_____
_____
_____
_____
_____
_____
_____
_____

"Be fruitful!"

I am the Fruit-Bearing Vine, and you are My branches that are filled with My life. I call you to bear fruit for the glory of My Father. It is the fruit produced not by religious striving or human manufacture, but the fruit of My Spirit. I call you to reflect Me with the fruit My Spirit produces through you.

The great strength of My Spirit will flow through you as you bring before Me a tender heart. Your works are powerless apart from Me. Your good deeds, though laudable before others, are only filled with power as you are filled with My Spirit. Be saturated to overflowing with My Spirit, and your very life will be a branch upon the Tree of Life.

I call you to love. I call you to joy. I call you to peace and gentleness and kindness and meekness. As you walk in self-control, My glory will flood your life with divine power to live in My realm. Be known as a person of tenderness before God. Many want to be correct, but I want you to be fruitful, with character and purity of heart. True beauty will enter your soul as you walk in the kindness and love of My Spirit. Others will see your beautiful life and know that it is the Father that is filling you with grace. I will be more than enough as you bring Me all of your heart. This is the day of being My fruitful one, My holy one, My glorious one. I am your God, and I will bring it to pass as you yield to Me.

JOHN 15:3–5

"The words I have spoken over you have already cleansed you. So enter into life-union with me, for I have entered into life-union with you. For as a branch severed from the vine will not bear fruit, so your life will be fruitless unless you live your life intimately joined to mine. I am the sprouting vine and you're my branches. As you live in union with me as your source, fruitfulness will stream from within you—but when you live separated from me you are powerless."

Reflect on the fruit of the Spirit (love, joy, peace, longsuffering, kindness, goodness, faithfulness, gentleness, self-control). List the fruit you'd like to see more of in your life and add a prayer of yielding to Him.

_____

_____

_____

_____

_____

_____

_____

_____

_____

_____

_____

_____

_____

_____

_____

"My love will guide you."

Do you love Me, My child? Is there a passion in your heart this day to do My will and follow My paths? All of heaven comes to your aid when you set your heart to pursue Me. I will guide you with My love.

Many on earth will value your life by what you do, your influence, your possessions, your ministry. But I value you and measure you by My love. All that I ask of you is what I asked of My servant Matthew, "Come, follow Me." As you walk with Me, our hearts beat as one, My pleasure rests upon you, and you begin to learn of My ways. The motives of your heart are changed from living for yourself to living for My glory and knowing My love.

My guidance is an expression of My love. Because I love you I will set you on high where none can hinder you or harm you. Because I love you I lead you into pleasant paths and go before you. My love will guide you, My child.

PSALM 91:14–16

"Because you have delighted in me as my great lover,
* I will greatly protect you.*
* I will set you in a high place, safe and secure before my face.*
I will answer your cry for help every time you pray,
* and you will find and feel my presence*
* even in your time of pressure and trouble.*
* I will be your glorious Hero and give you a feast!*
You will be satisfied with a full life and with all that I do for you.
* For you will enjoy the fullness of my salvation!"*

Today's entry reads like a love letter from your Savior.
Express your desire and passion for Him
with a love letter in return.

_____

_____

_____

_____

_____

_____

_____

_____

_____

_____

_____

_____

_____

_____

_____

_____

_____

_____

"I will free you when you give Me thanks!"

The power of gratitude has been undervalued by My people. As you give Me thanks, I refine your soul and remove regret from your life. I will free you when you give Me thanks. The more you are satisfied, the more freedom and release from pain I will bring into your life. The power of praise has yet to be fully activated. Greater than any force known to man is the power I release when you praise Me.

To receive My blessings and never give Me thanks is the mark of an unbeliever. To receive My blessings and be consumed with gratitude is the mark of a true worshipper. I call you to a life of gratitude. Many are like those who grumbled to Moses in the wilderness. They could not give Me praise. For even as they grumbled, My glory cloud was over their heads. They looked at man and not at Me! Ingratitude is a disease that is easily spread among My people. But praises will break the curse, lift the veil, open the heavens, and provide miracles even in a wilderness.

I call you to joy and thanksgiving! Let every day be the

day of magnificent praises! Lift up your eyes and see the blessings I have provided for you, and let the world know that you are Mine. The redeemed must say so by their thanks and by their extravagant praise. Today, set your heart before Me, Your Father, and learn the sweet lessons of gratitude. I will free you when you give Me thanks!

PSALM 136:1–5

Let everyone thank God, for he is good, and he is easy to please!
  His tender love for us continues on forever!
Give thanks to God, our King over all gods!
  His tender love for us continues on forever!
Give thanks to the Lord over all lords!
  His tender love for us continues on forever!
Give thanks to the only miracle working God!
  His tender love for us continues on forever!
Give thanks to the Creator who filled the heavens with revelation!
  His tender love for us continues on forever!

List at least five things you're truly thankful for today,
and feel your heart open to the release and peace
that only comes from Him.

_____

_____

_____

_____

_____

_____

_____

_____

_____

_____

_____

_____

_____

_____

_____

_____

_____

_____

"It takes courage to follow Me!"

Many have chosen the path of righteousness, only to discover that there is no room on the path for self-promotion and self-praise. It takes courage to follow Me! Those who follow Me find that I am enough. Everything is left behind when I stand before you. Come, follow Me, and you will be made into My likeness.

My Son is the Lamb slain before anything was created. He is more than the Lamb—He is the sacrificial Lamb. Born crucified, He lived before Me daily as My delight. We took pleasure and delight in one another. And I find My delight in you, for you also have been born crucified. As one with My Lamb, we will sit and rule together in eternal glory. Can you not leave behind what clings to your soul? Can your affections now burn with love for Me? It is more than a choice; it is courage that must fill your heart as you look upon the horizon. Never fear what is to come, for I am the One who was, who is, and who is to come!

You are an heir of the kingdom—all My promises to you are yes and amen! Nothing will disappoint you as you walk into My kingdom reality. Glory, ever-increasing glory, will surround you. To follow Me is not merely leaving everything; it is gaining everything. Set your gaze on what I am to you and what I have deposited inside your heart. All things are now yours: life, eternity, authority, power, and glory. No one will be able to take these from you. Move forward without fear, and I will be your great reward!

LUKE 5:10–11

Jesus answered, "Do not yield to your fear, Simon Peter. From now on you will catch men for salvation!" After pulling their boats to the shore, they left everything behind and followed Jesus.

Reflect on what He is to you and what He has deposited in your heart. What does walking with courage into His promises look like to you?

_____

_____

_____

_____

_____

_____

_____

_____

_____

_____

_____

_____

_____

_____

_____

_____

_____

"Heaven's gates are open to you!"

Lamb's blood has gone before you, My child. A blood-sprinkled path has been inaugurated and dedicated for you. Come into My glory! Expect a supernatural encounter in your life, for heaven's gates are open to you!

Many are content to remain outside, singing songs of praise, busy with a flurry of activities in My name, yet all the time heaven's gates are opened wide, ready for a throne-room encounter. Come up! Rest your weary soul, cease from striving to enter in, and simply come. The festive celebration awaits you! The feast of love has been prepared for My children. Your Father invites, yes, calls you to come! The call to enter in means all has been set in place, every veil taken away, and every obstacle to your faith has been removed. Heaven's gates are open to you!

Prayer is the path into My presence. Sacred blood is all the virtue that is required. For I have washed you, I have bathed you in My goodness, and I have cleansed the deepest place of your heart. You are My ready worshiper.

The bride doesn't gaze upon her bridal gown but upon her Beloved's face. It is not your holiness, but My grace that brings you in. Come closer and closer to Me, and I will come closer to you. Come with your heart swelling with faith and expectancy, and you will enter into a bliss that only My lovers experience. Come into My cloud-filled chamber, and I will cause all My goodness to pass before your eyes. Heaven's gates are open to you!

HEBREWS 10:19–20

And now we are brothers and sisters in God's family because of the blood of Jesus, and he welcomes us to come right into the most holy sanctuary in the heavenly realm— boldly and with no hesitation. For he has dedicated a new, a life-giving way for us to approach God. For just as the veil was torn in two, Jesus' body was torn open to give us free and fresh access to him!

Have you ever experienced a supernatural
encounter as you've rested in prayer and praise
in His presence? Recount your experience here,
and let it inspire you to draw closer to Him.

_____
_____
_____
_____
_____
_____
_____
_____
_____
_____
_____
_____
_____
_____
_____
_____
_____
_____

"I have made you rich."

I am your miracle Provider. I give to you all that you need to follow Me, to live in joy, and to excel in life. Count your blessings: joy unlimited, peace that prevails over every shadow, hope that will never dim. I give to you the wealth of eternity, for I live within your heart. I have made you rich!

There is no limit to My power to work on your behalf. You will never ask of Me something that goes beyond My ability to accomplish. All that you ask for, I will give to you as you come wrapped in My Son. Many focus their gaze only on their limitation, on what they feel is missing. But I call you, My child, to set your gaze upon Me and My limitless grace to provide all that you ask for. Is your family beyond My grace? Is My power and love enough to change them? Is your financial lack beyond My ability to give you all that you need? I have made you rich, and your wealth is not hidden; it is found in My Son. He made Himself poor so that through His "poverty" you might be made rich. The pastures of grace await your resting soul. Come and take your delight in the glory of My grace.

EPHESIANS 1:2–3

May God himself, the heavenly Father of our Lord Jesus Christ,
release grace over you and impart total well-being into your
lives. Everything heaven contains has already been lavished
upon us as a love gift from our wonderful heavenly Father, the
Father of our Lord Jesus—all because he sees us wrapped into
Christ. This is why we celebrate him with all our hearts!

Count your blessings today by writing them out.
Then write a statement of faith that He will give you
all that you ask for as you focus on Him.

_____

_____

_____

_____

_____

_____

_____

_____

_____

_____

_____

_____

_____

_____

_____

_____

_____

_____

_____

"I will blanket cities with My glory!"

I will bring a great and glorious move of My Holy Spirit. It is imminent. When your hearts break open to Me, I will break open the heavens over you! You will see with your eyes what I can do even in the darkness that seems to prevail around you. Nothing will hinder My strong arm as I penetrate darkness with My Spirit. Even as I brought the city of Nineveh to repentance and conversion, so I will blanket entire cities with My glory!

Believe and you will see! The move of My Spirit means that all things are possible. Watch what I will do with media, for they will broadcast to the nations the miracles of My hand. The Son of Glory will yet be famous again for His mighty works!

Praying men and women will partner with worshippers to bring an atmosphere over the cities. One city will remain in darkness while another will burst forth with light, life, and love! Am I not more than enough to do this? Many have longed to see what your eyes will soon witness. A hunger for My presence will consume you as I blanket cities with My glory.

Ask of Me, and I will give you cities of the nations as your inheritance! Ask in faith, knowing that there is no such thing as impossibility to Me! I will bring healing. And a river of salvation will flow in the cities of your nation.

PSALM 68:28–29

Display your strength, God, and we'll be strong!
  For your miracles have made us who we are.
  Lord, do it again,
  and parade from your temple your mighty power.
  By your command even kings will bring gifts to you.

Can you imagine how your city would look if it were blanketed by His glory? Take a moment to describe what would be different and better. Read your description aloud and pray, "Display your strength, God!"

_____

_____

_____

_____

_____

_____

_____

_____

_____

_____

_____

_____

_____

_____

_____

_____

"Wait on Me."

I have seen your love, your desire to please Me. Many times you have chosen Me above all else, and I am pleased. But you are growing weary. You have waited upon Me, and I say keep waiting on Me and I will not disappoint you.

What you call delay, I call preparation. Many times I am at work behind the scenes, yet you cannot discern it. I am preparing others so that your destiny may be fulfilled, and I am preparing you even as I prepared Joseph for his season of promotion. Never judge My works by what your eyes see but by the promises I have made to you. I *will* fulfill My word, and your eyes will see the miracles of My hand.

The days of completion are Mine, not yours. I will complete the work I have for you as My timing comes to pass. Even as My ways are perfect, so My timing is perfect. For you have said, "It seems I am standing still and going nowhere." But I say over you, I am unfolding My glory upon you even as you wait on Me. Join your heart to Mine. Entwine your heart into Mine, and you will see My glory, even in a season of waiting. Trust in Me and lay aside every anxiety and every form of impatience, and I will bring a miracle to pass in your life, for I am the Father of Love. I will make it happen and show you My perfection.

PSALM 13:5–6

Lord, I have always trusted in your kindness, so answer me.
  I will yet celebrate with passion and joy
  when your salvation lifts me up.
I will sing my song of joy to you, the Most High,
  for in all of this you have strengthened my soul.
  My enemies say that I have no Savior,
  but I know that I have one in you!

List a few areas of your life where you feel a "delay."
Then beside each, write what He says in response, such as
"I will not disappoint you"; "I will fulfill My word";
"My timing is perfect"; "Trust in Me." Whenever you
are tempted to impatience, repeat this exercise!

_____

_____

_____

_____

_____

_____

_____

_____

_____

_____

_____

_____

_____

_____

_____

"I will do the impossible for you."

The love I have for you is endless. It endures beyond the days of your life and finds its completion in eternity. My love has stepped out of heaven and stepped into your life. I will intensify your experience of My love as you seek more of Me. Is there something in front of you that looks impossible? Are the hearts of others unyielding to Me? Is your family surrounded by difficulty and stress? I will do the impossible for you, for My love will win the day!

What seems to be hard, I will make it easy for you. When it looks like everything has blocked your way and there is no one near you to help, I will make it easy for you. When it appears to you that you are always letting go and walking into more difficulty, I promise you, I will make it easy for you!

Grace will always empower you to sacrifice your personal wishes as you worship in My presence. Strength replaces weakness, grace floods into your impossibility, and I will make it easy for you. The burden you carry must be laid down as you take up My easy yoke and learn of Me. I will enrich your soul, enflame your heart, and give you a greater joy. Come into My sacred chamber, where every sacrifice becomes sweeter than honey and every loss becomes gaining more of Me.

I will do the impossible for you, for you are the focus of My attention and the apple of My eye. I will love you into victory until what seems to be hard becomes the way of grace and glory.

SONG OF SONGS 8:6–7

Place this fierce, unrelenting fire over your entire being.
Rivers of pain and persecution will never extinguish this flame.
Endless floods will be unable to quench this raging fire
  that burns within you.
Everything will be consumed.
It will stop at nothing as you yield everything to this furious fire
  until it won't even seem to you like a sacrifice anymore.

Song of Songs describes God's love for us as an unquenchable fire. Imagine standing before that fire and throwing in all of the impossibilities of your life. See them go up in flames! Write a prayer thanking Him that His yoke is easy and His burden is light.

_____

_____

_____

_____

_____

_____

_____

_____

_____

_____

_____

_____

_____

_____

_____

_____

_____

"I will finish the beautiful work I have begun in you!"

I have made you into My holy dwelling place. I have cleansed your heart and made you pure in My eyes. My holiness lives in you, for My Spirit lives in you. When you allow Me to fill you over and over, there is no evil that can touch you. When I reign as King of your life, your heart becomes the chamber room of My glory. I will finish the beautiful work I have begun in you!

Holiness is not a work or something you can produce. It does not originate with man, but it is a flow of My Spirit within you. What I cleanse, I fill. And what I fill is made holy. Remember how I have worked in your life through your journey with me. I strengthened you in weakness and held you in your pain. Many times I have lifted you higher and redeemed your days, filling them with joy. Never forget, My child—I will finish the beautiful work I have begun in you!

PHILIPPIANS 1:9–11

I continue to pray for your love to grow and increase more and more until it overflows, bringing you into the rich revelation of spiritual insight in all things. And with this revelation you will come to know God fully as he imparts to you the deepest understanding of his ways. This will enable you to choose the most excellent way of all—becoming pure and without offense until the unveiling of Christ. And you will be filled completely with the fruits of righteousness that are found in Jesus, the Anointed One—bringing great praise and glory to God!

Have you ever seen a work of art in progress? Sometimes it looks quite messy, doesn't it? But in the end something beautiful emerges as a result of the master's hand. Reflect on how you see Him working on the beautiful work that is you and your life.

"Rest in Me, O carrier of My glory."

I have longed to pour out upon you even more of My love and power. Can't you see that I have designed you as a carrier of My glory?

Come before Me this day and empty out your heart; pour it out at My feet, and I will fill you with such delight and joy that you will not be able to contain it. For I am building My church through the glory of My presence.

Stand in My presence until you know that I am your Strength. Even when the powers of darkness are around you on every side, you can be strong, for I have wrapped My glory-robe upon your soul and nothing will be able to harm you.

Gates of darkness will not prevail when I am near you. The days of heaven on earth are at hand. The days of the mighty moving of My Spirit will soon be seen by all. My powerful wind will blow away the clouds of doubt that have been over your mind and your heart. My glory-wind will make your enemies scatter, and you will stand complete and secure.

You will not be overcome by the fear that has overwhelmed many in this day, for I have made you an overcomer, a carrier of My glory.

Trust Me and watch Me fight for you. Lean into My heart and watch My love win every battle. Don't be disturbed by those who stumble, for they stumble in the darkness. I have become your Light and your Salvation, and you will have no fear. My love will keep you from stumbling. I have gone before you and made sure that your way is clear and your pathway secure, for I am your Father.

My plans for your life extend beyond your view, beyond your understanding of My ways. You see only what is in front of you today, but I have gone into your future and I know the good things that will unfold before you. Never doubt that your days are in My hands; rest in Me, O carrier of My glory, and watch Me fill you, protect you, and make you strong.

PSALM 25:4–5

Lord, direct me throughout my journey,
  so I can experience your plans for my life.
  Reveal the life-paths that are pleasing to you.
Escort me along the way, take me by the hand and teach me,
  for you are the God of my increasing salvation;
  I have wrapped my heart into yours!

Beginning with "Lord, direct me throughout my journey,"
write your own psalm asking the Lord to guide you and
show you the path He has cleared for you.

_____

_____

_____

_____

_____

_____

_____

_____

_____

_____

_____

_____

_____

_____

_____

_____

_____

_____

I hear His whisper ...

"Give your heart to Me."

Today you will see how vain the things of this life have become. Don't give your heart to the things of this world, but give your heart to Me. Don't live only for the pleasures of this life, but drink deeper from the river of pleasure called Eternal Life.

I give you a more pure fountain, a clear pool, a refreshing stream—it is not the muddy fountain of this world, but the crystal clear pool of My love for you.

Let nothing steal your heart but Me. I am aware of all that you need and I promised you, I will meet every need you have, even before you ask Me.

For My glory is My love for you. My honor is found in how I have treated you.

I am more interested in you than I am a thousand galaxies or a million stars. You mean more to Me than anything else I have created, for I gave sacred blood for you. Hear My voice today, not the sounds that originate on earth.

My voice will bring you to My presence, for I lead My sheep and they know My voice. Let your devotion to Me have no limit this day. Be willing to turn aside from the trivial to find the eternal. And I will make you a bright light in a dark place. You will become the sunrise of glory to many who sit in the dark shadows of despair.

As you set your heart on Me, hope will overflow from you to all your family and to all those who witness My blessings spilling from your life.

How will My message be heard without a messenger of My light? You will go with winged feet to carry the sounds of My voice to many people. So find rest in My heart. In this world there is little to soothe you, but in My heart you will discover My kindness to comfort you. So come away. Leave the vain things of this life behind and come to Me.

JOHN 10:14–15

"I alone am the Good Shepherd and I know those whose hearts are mine, for they recognize me and know me, just as my Father knows my heart and I know my Father's heart. I am ready to give my life for the sheep."

Look around at creation. You mean more to Him than anything else He created. What does that mean to you? Write a letter of devotion to Him.

_____

_____

_____

_____

_____

_____

_____

_____

_____

_____

_____

_____

_____

_____

_____

_____

_____

"I will keep My promise."

I have promised you that I would provide your every need. I have kept My promise and will keep it still.

I am the God who fed a million people in their wilderness journey, yet they complained and doubted Me over and over. You will see My hands opened to you, full of everything that you need.

The wilderness test has come. As I tested Phillip with the hungry multitude, I have tested your heart to see if you would look only to Me as your great supply and your great reward. I will bring My glory over all your disappointment and break your limitations as you look to Me. Never doubt in the dark what I have revealed to you in the light, for My promises endure and I have never failed to show you My love. Nourish your heart in My promises and laugh at your impossibilities, and the miracle will be birthed in your heart.

Stones will praise Me. Will you praise Me even before you see the miracle manifest? Watch Me work where you have given up hope. Watch what I will do when you fill your heart with praises. From the dark chaos I will bring forth beauty, abundant life, and radiant light. Even this day you will see the beginning of all I have planned for you when you look to Me and to Me alone.

HEBREWS 6:15–18

So Abraham waited patiently in faith and succeeded in seeing the promise fulfilled. It is very common for people to swear an oath by something greater than themselves, for the oath will confirm their statements and end all dispute. So in the same way, God wanted to end all doubt and confirm it even more forcefully to those who would inherit his promises. His purpose was unchangeable, so God added his vow to the promise. So it is impossible for God to lie for we know that his promise and his vow will never change! And now we have run into his heart to hide ourselves in his faithfulness. This is where we find his strength and comfort, for he empowers us to seize what has already been established ahead of time—an unshakeable hope!

Is there an area of your life where you feel tested or have been waiting for breakthrough for a long time? Remember His promises and write a prayer of praise to Him, thanking Him that He keeps His promises.

_____

_____

_____

_____

_____

_____

_____

_____

_____

_____

_____

_____

_____

_____

_____

_____

_____

"I will restore you."

Do not be afraid to follow Me into the unknown, for I am the one who leads you on and restores your life. I have placed within you My glorious treasure, and I care for you. This year will be a year of restoration in your life. You will be restored in My love, strengthened in My grace, and surrounded with songs of joy.

I will restore you. Never limit Me. I will restore your family and those you love. They will see Me in your life and know that I am the One who gives back to you what has been lost. Don't doubt My grace that is enough for you and for your family.

I say to you, I will restore you and provide for you in ways that will reveal My heart of love. My mercy brings gifts and surprises and supplies—all that you need. There will always be provision for your needs, and in My mercy I will reveal where you can find Me, for this will be the season of abundant supply for every need you have.

I will restore your mind and your heart as you come before Me. Crooked things will be made straight within you. For everything I do for you I do inside your heart, healing your spirit and soothing your soul. Come and find My heart, and I will restore your heart.

Greater passions will rise within you to feast upon My Word and drink of My Spirit. The hunger I give you will bring you deeper into My grace and My love for you.

I will restore your dreams. Those desires within you for completion and to touch the lives of others, I will fulfill. In the whispers of the night I will watch over every word I speak to you, and it will be fulfilled. You will see that My ways are perfect.

PSALM 51:12–14

Let my passion for life be restored,
  tasting joy in every breakthrough you bring to me.
  Give me more of your Holy Spirit-Wind
  so that I may stand strong and true to you!
Then I can show to other guilty ones
  how loving and merciful you are.
  They will find their way back home to you,
  knowing that you will forgive them.
O God, my saving God,
  deliver me fully from every sin,
  even the sin that brought blood-guilt to my soul.
  Then my heart will once again be thrilled to sing
  the passionate songs of righteousness and forgiveness!

God promises to restore your heart, mind, and dreams as well as provide for your physical needs. Prayerfully list out a few of your needs in each of these areas, and ask Him to show you how He wants to restore you.

_____

_____

_____

_____

_____

_____

_____

_____

_____

_____

_____

_____

_____

_____

_____

"My overcomers will rise."

The path I take you on is not the wide way that leads to destruction, but a narrow way that grows more narrow as I lead you forward. I must have My overcomers. I must have My daybreakers.

They will be those whom I take down narrow paths that lead into My heart and into My ways. Faith I will give you, but the good works you must do for Me will only come when ego is out of the way and left behind. My overcomers will rise and sing even when imprisoned and in pain.

I will come through you as a flood, washing away what defiles. At times, my flood will bring tears as you see how intent I am on making you My deliverer.

There is a place where My prisoners of love are kept close to My heart. And there nothing can disturb them, even when the earth is shaking all around them. I must have My overcoming ones, and My preparation of their hearts will be complete. For this is why your path grows more narrow, so narrow that only I will take you through.

With My love comes My power. You will no longer walk in your own way and the paths of your own choosing, for

I have destined you to reign in life as My overcomer, My dawnmaker. But for you to become My overcomer, I must first conquer you thoroughly and completely. Then you will rise like an eagle in the sky, unable to fall, for I will keep you from falling as you keep yourself in My love.

HEBREWS 13:20–22

Now may the God who brought us peace by raising from the dead our Lord Jesus Christ so that he would be the Great Shepherd of his flock; and by the power of the blood of the eternal covenant ... may he work perfection into every part of you giving you all that you need to fulfill your destiny. And may he express through you all that is excellent and pleasing to him through your life-union with Jesus the Anointed One who is to receive all glory forever! Amen!

Have you ever felt that the way God is leading you on is becoming more narrow, maybe even more painful? Has it occurred to you that He could be strengthening you to be His overcomer? Reflect on that idea here.

_____

_____

_____

_____

_____

_____

_____

_____

_____

_____

_____

_____

_____

_____

_____

_____

_____

"I close doors for you."

I will never disappoint you. Remember how I have helped you and held you in the past? I would not allow your enemies to conquer you. I broke through the clouds of despair and rescued you. I will not disappoint you. You are often disappointed when I close a door. Yet the door I close keeps you from making the wrong decision and taking the wrong path. Never lose heart when you see that I have shut a door. I open doors that no man can close and I close doors that no man can open. Can you praise Me when I close door as well as when I open a door?

The doors I close will prove to be a blessing to you. Let no disappointment come when I have chosen the best for you. The door shut before you gives you a greater opportunity to experience My best for your life. For I am in charge of your destiny and choose the right path when you surrender to Me. I will open the right door for every door I close, and you will see the wisdom of My love for you. I will not only bring you great joy but I will also spare you from needless pain. Believe in My love, rely on My love, and you will never be disappointed.

PSALM 18:30–31

What a God you are! Your path for me has been perfect!
   All your promises have proven true.
   What a secure shelter for all those
   who turn to hide themselves in you!
   You are the wraparound God giving grace to me.
Could there be any other god like you?
   You are the only God to be worshipped,
   for there is not a more secure foundation
   to build my life upon than you.

Can you think of a time when God closed a door but opened up a better path for you? Recount that situation here and praise Him for the closed doors.

_____

_____

_____

_____

_____

_____

_____

_____

_____

_____

_____

_____

_____

_____

_____

_____

_____

"You will be My instrument."

I will transform you and make you into a different person. As I train you to hear My voice, you will become a sharpened instrument in My hands. These are the days that I will train you and instruct you in My ways, giving you many secrets of what I am about to do. For I will make you a missionary of hope to many. You will be a voice that always brings life to others and grace to the weakest one. I will put words in your mouth that have never been declared or spoken before. I chose you for a purpose, and My plan for your life will be fulfilled.

Give Me a listening heart, and I will give you hope-filled words for what is to come. Many think they have heard My voice and have not. Some have heard My whisper but it has yet to change their heart. But I have called you with purpose to hear with clarity and to take My life-giving words and build up the lives of others. Even this day I will use you to strengthen what is feeble and to help the one who is brokenhearted. Listen carefully to My words, and you will be one who is fully equipped to represent Me.

You have said to Me, "Take my life and make me into the person You want me to be." Listen to My words, and they will be life and power inside of you. The greatest joy of your life will be in knowing Me—that I am kind, tenderhearted to My children, and full of compassion and forgiveness toward those who fall.

I will make you a sharpened, pure instrument of mature love. Bring to Me your listening heart, and I will bring to you the life and change you long for.

PROVERBS 8:32–35

So listen, my sons and daughters to everything I tell you,
  for nothing will bring you more joy than following my ways.
Listen to my counsel for my instruction will enlighten you.
  You'll be wise not to ignore it!
If you wait at wisdom's doorway,
  longing to hear a word for every day,
  joy breaks forth within you as you listen for what I'll say.
For the fountain of life pours into you every time that you find me,
  and this is the secret of growing in the delight
  and the favor of the Lord!

Take a moment to listen to what
He wants to say to you today. Record the words
He has for you or someone else.

_____

_____

_____

_____

_____

_____

_____

_____

_____

_____

_____

_____

_____

_____

_____

_____

_____

_____

"I will speak to you."

In the silence I will speak to you. Each morning, come and sit at My feet and learn from the wisdom of eternity. I will whisper to your soul. It is time for you to hear Me clearly each day. The task I set before you will bring sweetness to your soul. Others will begin to take note that you have been with Me.

In the evening hours, come to Me and I will whisper My living words into your spirit. I will make your night season a time of encounter as My Spirit comes to bring you heaven's grace and the dew of My presence. Listen carefully, as a lover listens to every word of the Beloved—listen to Me and you will hear My voice. I will touch your ears and open them as one who is being taught. You will learn My ways as you listen to My voice.

I love to speak with you, to talk to you and share My heart with you. I have many who say they follow Me but never still their souls to listen to My voice. I am a Shepherd who goes before My sheep, calling them by name, caring for them in love, and leading them into My ways. You will find that I have ears for your voice; I listen to you as you speak with Me. Now come and listen to My whisper each day and know that I am your God.

PROVERBS 8:8–12

All the declarations of my mouth can be trusted;
  they contain no twisted logic or perversion of the truth.
All my words are clear and straightforward to everyone
  who possess spiritual understanding.
  If you have an open mind, you'll receive revelation-knowledge.
My wise correction is more valuable than silver or gold.
  The finest gold is nothing compared
  to the revelation-knowledge I can impart.
Wisdom is so priceless that it exceeds the value than any jewel.
  Nothing you could wish for can equal her.
For I am wisdom, and I am shrewd and intelligent.
  I have at my disposal living-understanding
  to devise a plan for your life.

How can you create space in your life this week
to simply sit and listen to God? Make a plan here,
and see what He reveals to you in the quiet.

_____

_____

_____

_____

_____

_____

_____

_____

_____

_____

_____

_____

_____

_____

_____

_____

"Remain faithful to Me."

The word I speak to you today is *endurance*. I call you to be faithful unto the end, even as I loved My disciples unto the end. The burden you carry must always be brought to the cross and left forever at My feet. Others will not understand the load you carry and the secret woundings of your soul, but I understand. You must never compare yourself to another, but bring your cares to the One who cares. You will never be asked to carry more than you can endure, but it will be more than you think. I call you to stretch your faith until it is greater than your burden.

I have called you to be a faithful warrior of My love. The woundings of your soul bring you into deeper love. You see the momentary pain, but I see the blossoms of love beginning to open within you, yielding a sweeter fragrance. Even when you feel disappointed, My love never fails. When you are wounded by love, My mercy still stands higher than the heavens. I call you to hold every experience of your life as sacred, and then you will discover My goodness and My power to work everything together for good as you love Me.

Speak over your life this day these words: "I will endure all things for love."

As you remain faithful to Me, love grows within you. My love and My peace will be the twin fruits from the Tree of Life to sustain you and sweeten your joy. Let nothing deter you from your pursuit of My face. Those who love Me most I will transform the most. Let every opportunity that comes to you this day be the open doorway into My presence.

I speak over you, My faithful one, endure all things for love as a good soldier of Jesus Christ, and always set His faithfulness before your eyes as your supreme example. And then you will not fail and you will not stumble. For I will hold you in My love even as I held Him in My love throughout His ordeals. I am with you and will exchange your weakness for My strength as you wait upon Me.

2 TIMOTHY 2:3–5

Overcome every form of evil as a victorious soldier of Jesus the Anointed One. For every soldier called to active duty must divorce himself from the distractions of this world so that he may fully satisfy the one who chose him. An athlete who doesn't play by the rules will never receive the trophy, so remain faithful to God!

Reflect on the trials Jesus endured for love.
List some of them here and meditate on how
He overcame them. After each meditation, speak aloud,
"I will endure all things for love."

_____

_____

_____

_____

_____

_____

_____

_____

_____

_____

_____

_____

_____

_____

_____

_____

_____

"My life is victory in you."

The victory I call you to walk in is within you. When nothing seems easy around you, I give you an easy victory within you. Yield to My life within, and you will find grace in every difficulty. My promise is a promise of victory, and My victory is My life released in you. I dispense My glory into you when you open your heart deeper to Me. Taste of My victory and rest in Me, for I have overcome all things.

I have brought you to this place because of My passionate and tender love for you. I want to show you My victory. I want you to learn of Me and take My easy yoke upon your soul and find rest in Me. Have I not promised to lead you to the quiet brooks of peace? I will show you the path as you still your heart before Me. Trust in Me and not in what you see. Believe in Me when fear attempts to stop your advance, and you will find My oasis of victory. Even when you don't know what to do or what step to take, My peace will guide you.

Keep your soul at rest. Let nothing disturb the hiding place of victory within you. My gift is victory today. My promise is victory tomorrow. How you rest in My victory today will enable Me to give you even more of My life tomorrow. Take My gift of today's victory and be content as I prepare tomorrow's triumph.

HEBREWS 4:1–3

Now God has offered to us the same promise of entering into his realm of resting in confident faith. So we must be extremely careful to ensure that we all embrace the fullness of that promise and not fail to experience it. For we have heard the good news of deliverance just as they did, yet they didn't join their faith with the Word and activate its power. Instead, what they heard didn't affect them deeply, for they doubted. For those of us who believe, faith activates the promise and we experience the realm of confident rest!

Do you believe that you have the victory within you today?
Reflect on what it means to rest in today's victory
and be content in His victory for tomorrow.

_____

_____

_____

_____

_____

_____

_____

_____

_____

_____

_____

_____

_____

_____

_____

_____

_____

"I will heal you."

I will heal you. I am moved by your cry and will answer when you ask Me to draw near. I will never close My eyes to your suffering, and I will never close My heart to your pain.

I am the Father of Encouragement and the God of all comfort. There is no part of you that I cannot touch and heal. I invite you to enter into My stronghold, My dwelling place of beauty and fix your eyes on Me.

As you gaze upon Me and drink of My Spirit, My healing power is released within you. My children are loved beyond understanding, and I demonstrate My love every moment. My healing light streams from above, and My healing grace floods your heart when you turn to Me. Everything I am is everything you need.

I am eager to share My life with you. The help that I give you is My life within you. My life is healing, strength, wisdom, and power. Lay hold of My life, eternal life, and you will find that everything changes. Come today. Come closer to Me, for I am your Healer, your Father, your Hiding Place.

PSALM 103:1–5

With my whole heart, with my whole life,
  and with my innermost being,
  I bow in wonder and love before you, the Holy God!
Yahweh, you are my soul's celebration.
  How could I ever forget the miracles of kindness
  you've done for me?
You kissed my heart with forgiveness, in spite of all I've done!
  You've healed me inside and out from every disease!
You've rescued me from hell and saved my life!
  You've crowned me with love and mercy and made me a king!
You satisfy my every desire with good things!
  You've supercharged my life so that I soar again
  like a flying eagle in the sky!

Where do you need healing in your life today?
Pour out your heart to Him here. Envision hiding in Him
and His healing grace flooding your heart.

_____

_____

_____

_____

_____

_____

_____

_____

_____

_____

_____

_____

_____

_____

_____

_____

_____

_____

_____

"I desire your praises."

Angels listen for your songs. Your songs of praise awaken the worship of angels. Your songs of worship bring the cries of "Holy" into My ears. Give me the deepest place of your spirit, and I will give you the deepest place of My love. Come within the chamber room of My delight and let Me hear your voice, for your voice is sweet and your face is lovely as you worship Me. My angels come to your gatherings because your love songs bring them near. Sing with all your heart, sing your love songs, and the angels will join you in worship and adoration.

Receive Me once again. Drink of Me and take Me in. Never say, "I have enough," for I always have more to give you. Like a cup receives the wine, receive My love as I pour it into your soul. The healing you long for will not come without the worship that I long for.

Soar into My glory with the wings of worship. Abandon your spirit to Me as a sail abandons itself to the wind. Let faith reenergize your affections toward Me. For did I not say that the love of many will grow cold? Be on fire with passion for Me, and you will discover My plans for your life. Shake off your soul passivity and lukewarm faith, for I am a God of consuming flames.

The revival of awakened hearts comes through praise. There is a secret power released when you bring high praises to Me. The power that shut the mouths of lions was the power of praise through the faith-filled lips of My servant Daniel. You will see many breakthroughs and many enemies silenced as you bring your sacred praises to Me. Angels are waiting to hear your chorus of praise. Activate the power of heaven by the high praise of your lips. These are the sacrifices I desire. More than money or time or talents, I desire your praises. For in your praise the glory descends.

PSALM 149:1–2

Hallelujah! Praise the Lord!
It's time to sing to God a brand new song,
so that all his holy people will then hear how wonderful he is!
May Israel be enthused with joy all because of him,
and may the sons of Zion pour out
their joyful praises to their King!

Write out a worship song you have memorized,
or write your own unique song of praise. Then read
(or sing) it aloud. Put your heart into it and feel His joy!

_____

_____

_____

_____

_____

_____

_____

_____

_____

_____

_____

_____

_____

_____

_____

_____

_____

"You are hidden in Christ."

Once I walked past a man. He could not see My face, so I hid him in the cleft of the rock. My servant Moses was My friend and holy partner. Yet I will not walk past you; you will see My face in Jesus Christ. In the wounds of His side I have placed you. And now your life is hidden, not in a rock, but in Christ.

The glory of My Son is now within you. This living Hope will keep you strong when others fall away, for you are inside of Me.

You will not be disappointed when you trust in Me. Everything about Me is life and love and peace. To rest in My life is your Sabbath delight. Only in Me will you find the treasures of wisdom and true knowledge. You can pass through the most difficult season of life and still find peace at the center of your spirit, for there I am. Did not My Son sleep at peace in the middle of a storm? The peace that is found in My voice will change the atmosphere around you.

In this hidden place, confusion and turmoil cannot exist. The glory of My life calms every storm and quiets every distraction. It is "little faith" that keeps you from finding this serenity. Great faith can move the mountains of fear and find peace in the raging winds. In this quiet place, the beauty of My forever love will change you. Garments of splendor will replace the rags of self. You will sit enthroned with Me in the highest place, hidden from the dark powers of earth. Come and seek Me with all your heart. I will not hide from you, but I will hide you in Me.

COLOSSIANS 3:2–4

Yes, feast on all the treasures of the heavenly realm and fill your thoughts with heavenly realities, and not with the distractions of the natural realm. Your crucifixion with Christ has severed the tie to this life, and now your true life is hidden away in God as you live within the Anointed One. And every time Christ himself is seen for who he really is, who you really are will also be revealed, for you are now one with him in his glory!

What does it mean to you to be hidden in Christ? Write about some of the "heavenly realities" that are yours as a result of being seated with Him on high.

_____

_____

_____

_____

_____

_____

_____

_____

_____

_____

_____

_____

_____

_____

_____

_____

_____

_____

"I will work through you."

I love you in your struggle and weakness. While you are still far off, I run to you in restoration. While you are still speaking your words of repentance, I am forgiving you. While you are pondering your future, I have gone before you to open up the way. While you are asleep, I place My grace over you. While you hope that your family is healed, I am at work in hearts to make you whole.

Within you is a deep need. That need is for My grace and mercy.

More than a companion to you, I will be strength and grace in your every moment. Not one thing will keep Me from cleansing you and empowering you in My grace. I will use you even in your weakness to bring healing to your family. Look to Me and hope in Me. Place all your expectations in Me, and I will never disappoint you. Do not expect your family to change, but expect Me to change your heart and then I will change your family and bring them to Me.

Every time you feel this deep need, receive more of My grace. Like a river that always seeks the lowest place, My grace runs down into the deepest need of your heart and fills it to overflowing. Soon you will leap over every way and run victoriously through the ranks of the enemy's forces that have come against you. I will train you in My grace to win every battle and defeat the discouragement that has sought to muffle your voice. You will rise and run into My grace and find all that you need, for I am the extravagant Father who understands you fully. So come and expect Me, the faithful One, to work through you to change the world around you.

2 TIMOTHY 1:12

The confidence of my calling enables me to overcome every difficulty without shame, for I have an intimate revelation of this God. And my faith in him convinces me that he is more than able to keep all that I've placed in his hands safe and secure until the fullness of his appearing.

What are those things you want to place "in His hands safe and secure until the fullness of His appearing"? Commit them afresh in His care.

_____

_____

_____

_____

_____

_____

_____

_____

_____

_____

_____

_____

_____

_____

_____

_____

_____

_____

_____

"Holy fire will fall."

My fire is coming to consume and purify your heart. Holy fire is about to fall upon you and all those who long for Me. It is the fire of cleansing that I have reserved for those who love Me. You have passed through fire before and it left you strong. That was My fire of testing. For all who desire Me will be tried by fire.

You have walked through the fire of misunderstanding and remained at My side through it all. But this fresh fire I will release to the earth is a fire that will cling to your soul and make you whole. It is fire power, the power you need to bring My glory to the cities of the earth—this is what I am about to impart.

Many who have resisted My fire will fall away in the coming days. Have I not said that My angels are swift winds and My priests a blazing fire? Do I not send you out as flames to consume the hearts of men? Do not put out the Spirit's fire or resist the power and gifts that I give you. For My Spirit fire will conquer cities and bring them to the feet of Jesus, My King.

Every day passes and becomes a memory, but My living presence is eternal, for I dwell among the eternal flames of fire. Torches of fire burn before My throne, the seven spirits of God. They have been sent out into all the earth to baptize My people with power and anoint My servants. Embrace the fire I give to you, and you will receive power to endure and overcome the evil of this age. You have not yet seen what I will do with a generation that burns holy for Me.

HEBREWS 1:7

And about his angels he says, "I make my angels swift winds, and my ministers fiery flames!"

Write a prayer inviting the power and
the gifts that come through His fire.

_____

_____

_____

_____

_____

_____

_____

_____

_____

_____

_____

_____

_____

_____

_____

_____

_____

_____

"These are days of My cleansing grace."

I am cleansing you over and over and over—washing you in My love and soaking you in My grace. It is true that you are already clean, for the Word of God lives in you and brings forth fruit. But did I not wash My beloved disciples' feet? Many times your thoughts need My cleansing fire to destroy the lies that seek to lodge in your heart. I will cleanse your thoughts until you will be fixed only on the ways of holiness and purity. I will wash the defilement from your feet until every place you stand will become holy. I set you apart to be fully Mine, and what is it that makes you fully Mine? A surrendered heart and a mind that will carry My thoughts and bring them in love to others.

The sifting of your motives will continue until your conscience is clean before Me. I desire purity, not only outwardly, but with every activity of your life as you walk with motives that are right. Whatever you do, do it as unto Me. Whatever you speak, speak it as the living truths of God. Be wise and alert to the deception that is the greatest deception of all: self-deception.

As you go farther on My holy paths, you will see how I have placed truth deep inside you. You will not follow the crooked ways of using your gift for the admiration of others. You will lay down your crown, your gifts, and your meager substance at My feet, and I will make it holy. Even as I turned a serpent into the rod of God for Moses, I will take crooked things within you and grace you with My authority and presence until even your weakness has become strength before Me.

Move forward, set your eyes on destiny, and I will bring it to pass. Others may stop on their journey and take steps of selfishness, but you, My holy one, you will walk and not faint nor be distracted, for the prize of My glory is set before you. Come with Me, and I will make you faithful and true.

JOB 5:19

He will deliver you from trouble again and again. No matter what you go through he will rescue you, protecting you from injury.

We are often like the disciples, not wanting Jesus
to wash our feet but not realizing how much we need
His cleansing in order to reach our destiny.
Write a prayer of surrender to Him.

_____

_____

_____

_____

_____

_____

_____

_____

_____

_____

_____

_____

_____

_____

_____

"I bring you courage."

I come with a gift this day. I bring you courage, fresh courage. You must have strength to discover the riches and glory that I have deposited within you. Many are content with what their eyes behold, but you have asked Me for more. I see the willingness of your heart to leave the ordinary behind and find the supernatural wealth of My life. So I bring to you the living energy of faith, which is courage.

My love for you will never leave you defenseless. So do not set your gaze on the enemies of faith, for they will stumble and fall. You will rise with fresh courage and feast upon the reality of My presence at all times. For your true comfort and joy is not merely in the victory I give you, but in the One who calls you to be Mine. A bold courage to move forward in spite of what your eyes see is the gift you must take for this day. Lay hold of eternal life deep within you, and the power of that life will flow through you.

This I am doing for you as you have asked—I give you fresh vision for the future, filled with hope and courage to move forward. Every gift I bring must be received and utilized in your journey. So step out in faith and obedience to My Word, and you will find everlasting arms holding you and giving you strength. I come with My sword drawn, ready to fight for you, as you take your place at My feet in worship. Your earthly fears will be dissolved as you bow in fear of Me alone. I will guide you in the paths of righteous courage until you stand unashamed in My sacred presence.

JOHN 16:33

"And everything I've taught you is so that the peace which is in me will be in you and will give you great confidence as you rest in me. For in this unbelieving world you will experience trouble and sorrows, but you must be courageous, for I have conquered the world!"

He stands to fight for you and defend you as you worship Him. Envision Him surrounding you, with His sword drawn, everywhere you go. How does this encourage you? Write a response to this promise.

_____

_____

_____

_____

_____

_____

_____

_____

_____

_____

_____

_____

_____

_____

_____

_____

_____

"My love for you is great!"

Receive even more of My love. Drink it into your innermost being. My love is what transforms you and changes your thinking, your prayers, and the essence of your life. It is impossible for you to understand the depth of My love, for it is more than you can imagine and more than you can ever perceive. It will take eternity for you to even begin to grasp the wonder of My love for you. It is not meant to be a doctrine or a teaching. It is through every painful incident and every broken relationship I have felt. My heart is one with you and it is impossible for you to endure pain and I not endure it with you. I have never regretted for a moment My choice of you!

Look into the sky and see the vastness of My universe, yet My love is greater still. The universe cannot contain the depths of My love for you. I created all things as a gift for you. It is nothing compared to the joy I experience when I have you and when you come to be with Me. I laid aside My robes of glory to come and purchase you with My blood. You are the pearl of great price, and I sold all that I had to purchase you. You are the treasure hidden in the field. I came into this world and found you. Never doubt My love or allow its fire to dim in your heart. Stir up your heart to know My love and experience My endless delight of you.

PSALM 19:1–4

God's splendor is a tale that is told;
  his testament is written in the stars.
  Space itself speaks his story every day
  through the marvels of the heavens.
  His truth is on tour in the starry-vault of the sky,
  showing his skill in creation's craftsmanship.
Each day gushes out with glory to the next,
  night with night whispering its secret.
Without a sound, without a word, without a voice being heard,
Yet all the world can see its story.
  Everywhere its gospel is clearly read so all may know.

He cries with you in your pain and rejoices with you in your joy. He loves you more than you know! Write a thankful response to His endless delight of you.

_____

_____

_____

_____

_____

_____

_____

_____

_____

_____

_____

_____

_____

_____

_____

"I am building your life into a masterpiece of love."

Just as a builder lays a foundation for a large and strong house, I have laid a deep foundation in your life. This foundation is built upon the Rock of Truth. I have set up your walls and strengthened your being. You will be a stronghold of My presence, and I will display you to the world as My beautiful, artistic masterpiece!

Sacred blood I gave for you. Holy hands were opened to receive your nails. Beautiful feet that walked the streets of Jerusalem were pierced so that you would walk the streets of holiness with Me. I will bring My plans to pass. My longings for your life will be fulfilled. Do not look at the structure and say that it is inferior.

Look at My wisdom and say, "You do all things well." Even now I am preparing the next steps of your journey with Me. I am building you into a house of glory that I might show My overcoming, conquering strength on your behalf. Slowly and carefully, as the Master Builder I have constructed you and built you up. The superstructure is now seen, and I will finish what I have begun.

Many times you have asked Me, "Why does this take so long?" I speak to you this day: believe in My wise plan for your life, look to Me and it will come to pass. My power and grace will rise up within you, and what now seems impossible will be lifted from you. Your limitations are invitations for My power to deliver you. I will never fail you or disappoint you. My promises are rainbows of hope that cover you. My declarations over your life are greater than your heartache. Your tears are liquid words that I read and understand. Never doubt My conquering love, for I have determined to build you up into a spiritual house filled with trust, hope, and love.

PSALM 38:9

*Lord God, you know all my desires and my deepest longings.
My tears are liquid words and you can read them all.*

Stand back and look at your life as if it were
a building being constructed. Can you see His wise
plan coming together? Reflect on His faithfulness
to you throughout the different stages of your life.

_____

_____

_____

_____

_____

_____

_____

_____

_____

_____

_____

_____

_____

_____

_____

_____

_____

"Look through My eyes."

Come and look on My face. Gaze into My glory until you are transformed. I will give you new eyes, *My eyes*, which will give you true understanding. I call you to look through My eyes. When you look through My eyes, the world around you will change. When you see the sick, I see them healed. When you see the lost, I see them asleep and ready to be awakened. When you see darkness approaching, I see the enemy defeated. And when I look at you I see you completed, made whole and beautiful, with nothing lacking.

I call you into *true vision* that you might see. Buy from Me healing eye salve, and your vision will be clear. I will heal your eyes and cause you to clearly evaluate and discern the day in which you are living. Many see doom; I see glory. Many see devastation; I see My kingdom increasing and having no end. I see the end from the beginning, and when you come before My throne you will see what My prophet Isaiah saw—the whole earth is full of My glory!

From today forward I am calling you to lay aside your blindness and take My healing eye salve, the revelation of My love, and see everything differently. You will be known as sons and daughters of the Living God as you speak with purity and clear vision. I will show you the secrets of what is to come when your eyes have been healed and you look upon My throne. I give you this day *true vision* that springs from revelation and understanding. Your eyes will be anointed to see beyond the moment and call things that are not as though they are. I have given you this gift of discerning grace that you might bring hope where others have lost courage. Take this healing eye salve of love to the people, and watch what I will do as you speak My words and see with My eyes.

LUKE 8:17

Because this revelation lamp now shines within you, nothing will be hidden from you—it will all be revealed. Every secret of the kingdom will be unveiled and out in the open, made known by the revelation light.

Can you imagine what it would be like to see
the world and yourself through His eyes?
Compose a prayer asking Him to give you that true vision.

_____

_____

_____

_____

_____

_____

_____

_____

_____

_____

_____

_____

_____

_____

_____

_____

_____

"Rest at My side."

Heaven has opened its doors to receive you, for I have seated you with Me in the heavenly realm where we rest as One. I see you next to Me, no longer struggling to get My attention. You are in the place of rest at My side. This will transform you as you consider what it means to be one with Me. All that has troubled you cannot enter; the door is shut to the temporal and momentary. Eternity is within your heart, for I have come to be one with you.

I long to teach you what it means to be a son, a daughter of the Living God. Do not let your experience with an earthly father blind your eyes to who I am. You have a Father in heaven with a burning love for you. I have cherishing love for you, and I will give you the fruits of sonship. Let Me teach you the secrets of what it means to be My child. I will heal you of the pain that has prevented you from knowing Me fully.

Your life is about to change as you take your place at My right hand. I have made you holy in My presence. Absorb the glory that is around you, until you know that I am near. I have planted seeds in your life long ago that are just now starting to grow. There will be a paradise garden in your heart as My Spirit brings these dormant seeds to life and to fruitfulness. You will forget all your affliction and pain as you see the garden grow and release life inside your soul. You will radiate My glory and taste My goodness.

I have chosen you and could never forget the adoring worship you have poured out before Me. I am near to you even now, for My work is swiftly taking place in your life. I will complete this beautiful work inside your heart until you awaken with My likeness. Come and rest at My side until your eyes open to see Me face to face.

SONG OF SONGS 6:5

Turn your eyes from me, I can't take it anymore!
I can't resist the passion of the eyes that I adore.
Overpowered by a glance, my ravished heart—undone,
held captive by your love, I'm truly overcome!

Imagine yourself sitting at His right hand, just resting and looking at Him. How does it feel to know you are His child and He is your Father who cherishes you?

_____

_____

_____

_____

_____

_____

_____

_____

_____

_____

_____

_____

_____

_____

_____

_____

"I am preparing you."

I am training you and preparing you for the coming days. Your calling is unique and so your preparation will be unique. Nothing can hinder what I am preparing you for. You will experience all that I have planned—the fullness of My power is coming to you!

Soon, very soon, you will be astounded at the changes I have brought in your life. You will move from being in shadows to living in the brilliance of My glory. You will move from being confused to being comforted and filled with My life. Why would you doubt My plan for your life? Joseph would have never come to the place of ruling and reigning if he lived in doubt, even in the dark days of his prison. Yet you can see how My preparation of Joseph, My servant, was one of a kind. So will your preparation be unusual.

I am calling you to a wonderful place of influence as you touch the lives of many. Do not judge My plans for your life by the momentary mess that is around you or the unusual situation you find yourself in this day. I trained Moses to be My leader, My champion, on the backside of the desert. I trained David to be a warrior on the lonely hillside as he sang his psalms of praise to Me. I trained John the Baptist in the barren wilderness.

Will you desire Me at any cost? I will move in mystery to bring you into greater light. Trust until the light of a new day dawns. My mighty grace is given to you in your difficulties and in your delights. The grace I give to you cannot be diminished by what seems to be a delay. Trust, and the light will shine. Believe, and understanding will soon follow. I am all you need. In every step you take, let your heart say, "You are all I need!"

PROVERBS 4:4–6

"Never forget my words.
  If you do everything that I teach you, you'll reign in life!"
So make wisdom your quest—
  search for the revelation of life's meaning.
  Don't let what I say go in one ear and out the other!
Stick with wisdom and she will stick to you,
  protecting you throughout your days.

Have you doubted that your "unusual situation" could be His preparation for your place of influence? Reflect on the stories of Moses, David, and John the Baptist and write a statement of trust in Him.

_____

_____

_____

_____

_____

_____

_____

_____

_____

_____

_____

_____

_____

_____

_____

"Your Bridegroom is coming."

I am about to flow through your life in great power.
The age of miracles and displays of power will be seen in
your land. Even now My winds are blowing to topple the
structures and teachings of men that hinder My people from
trusting in My power. Gale force winds will blow. The more
confidence you place in the structures of men, the more
disappointment will come when I blow them down. So arise
from your days of doubting and enter in to a new day of
promises fulfilled, the days of heaven on earth!

Your Bridegroom is coming; He is in the land to lift you
up and lead you out. Trim your lamps, buy oil of My Spirit,
fill your heart with expectancy, and go out to meet Him.
The day of His wedding is near—arise and go out of all
that is familiar and meet Him in His glory. Just as He walks
in mighty power over all His foes, so will His bride walk in
the ways of glorious power. Nothing will hinder Him as He
appears for His bride.

I will speak My words through you, and I will release
My power through you. For the Lamb's wife is making
herself ready, and her garments of splendor are becoming

clean and spotless. I will draw untold millions to Myself in these days of power. So come, be clothed with faith and confidence in Me. Leave all that hinders you behind. Do not look back or try to take the old with you into the new. For the way is straight and the door is narrow. Come with faith alone, and you will see the unveiling of My power. There is no limit to what I will do through you as you come with Me!

SONG OF SONGS 3:10–11

The place where they sit together is sprinkled with crimson.
Love and mercy cover this carriage,
blanketing his tabernacle-throne.
The king himself has made it
for those who will become his bride!
Rise up Zion maidens, brides-to-be!
Come and feast your eyes on this king
as he passes in procession on his way to his wedding!
This is the day filled with overwhelming joy—
the day of his great gladness!

The Bridegroom is coming!
Do you feel Him preparing you? Does this fill you with joy?
Describe what you imagine it will be like when He comes.

_____

_____

_____

_____

_____

_____

_____

_____

_____

_____

_____

_____

_____

_____

_____

_____

_____

_____

"I am the Finisher!"

Today you stand at the threshold of a new beginning.
All that is around you will change, and all that I have
planted within you will now grow and bear fruit. For I
have great things in store for you, things no one has ever
proclaimed to you. Many speak of the rain that will soon
fall, but I say, it will be a *downpour* on you! Many speak of
the fire, but they have never been consumed. But with you,
My fire will rage and not be contained by the structures and
theories of men.

There are many who wish for a new day, but you will be
lifted suddenly into a season beyond your imagination or
your dreams. For it will be My dream that will be fulfilled in
your life. Many scoffers will be swept into My presence and
become believers in one day. Many doubters of My power
will leave their limitations and pursue Me as never before.
The time of the great outpouring upon the nations is near.
It will be a day of repentance and a day of gathering. Those
who ignore My truth will be ignored. Those who refuse to
gather themselves together will be scattered even farther.
For I will be worshipped in spirit and in truth.

So stand firm in Me until I have become your confidence. Set your eyes upon Me and don't be worried about your future and your calling, for I am the God who begins and completes, the Alpha and the Omega. You have seen Me many times as the Beginning—now you will see me as the Finisher!

PHILIPPIANS 1:6

I pray with great faith for you, because I'm fully convinced that the One who began this glorious expression of grace in you will faithfully continue the process of maturing you through your union with him and will complete it at the unveiling of our Lord Jesus Christ!

List some things that you believe God has begun in your life and that you look forward to Him finishing. Write a prayer asking Him to show you His dream for your life.

_____

_____

_____

_____

_____

_____

_____

_____

_____

_____

_____

_____

_____

_____

_____

_____

_____

_____

_____

"You are in Christ."

I will treat you as I treat My Son, for I have placed you in Him, My Beloved. You will face Me and look upon Me as My cherished one, for I will treat you with the favor that Jesus deserves. He has taken all that you deserved and carried it as His cross to Calvary. Now I will take all that He deserves and place it upon you. I have placed you in Him so that I can treat you like Him.

Inside of My heart you abide. I have placed you inside the relationship I have with My Son and Spirit. I have fully accepted you in the Beloved. My endless love is now toward you with the same strength that it is toward My Son. Though your heart is dull and so slowly does My light penetrate, yet cling to these words: I love you with the love I have for My Son, for you are in Him forever.

With the grace of Christ within you, soon you will do the works of Jesus. This will cause heaven to rejoice as My sons and daughters find their delight in seeing Me work through them. The miracles of My love will be seen through your life. As you discover the strength of My eternal love, all that is within you will be transformed. For I will have a people that reflect the glory of My Son. I will treat you with the favor that Jesus deserves. This is My glory and this is your destiny.

JOHN 1:18

No one has ever gazed upon the fullness of God's splendor,
*   except the uniquely beloved Son who is cherished by the Father*
*   and held close to his heart.*
*   Now he leads the way to the place of honor*
*   at the Father's side!*

God looks at you and sees Jesus. You are in Him!
Write a response to this wonderful truth.

_____

_____

_____

_____

_____

_____

_____

_____

_____

_____

_____

_____

_____

_____

_____

_____

"Set your heart on Me."

When you see something inside your soul that you lack, focus on Me. I am to be the center on which your life turns. Set your heart on Me and not on the petty offenses that come between you and another. My love will erase and cover a multitude of sins. When My Spirit fills you, every other thing is swept away and forgotten. This is how My persecuted ones endure—for they set their focus on My love.

The shining of My love upon you is the Light that guides, warms, nourishes, and strengthens. Turn your heart to the light of My love, and I will pull the "weeds" from your garden that hinder our fruit from coming forth. When you turn to Me, I will accomplish what all your strivings have not—I will change you from the inside out. I am patient and kind, and there is so much more compassion in My heart toward you than you have realized. You are not a disappointment to Me, but a delight!

Remember the price I paid to purchase your soul. I have given My Son for you. When you feel that I am distant, bathe your heart once again in My love and push aside the lies that would deceive you. I know you, I understand the moving of your heart, and I know every word you will speak before you even start a sentence. The pleasure I find in you is not because of your works, but because of your love. Having never seen Me, yet you love Me. I will never leave you nor diminish the strength of My love toward you.

Whenever you turn your focus to Me and set your gaze on things above, I am stirred to bring you into greater measures of My love and holiness. Let nothing silence your songs of praise, and let nothing stand in your way as you pursue the quest for even more of My love.

COLOSSIANS 2:14–15

And through the divine authority of his cross, he cancelled out every legal violation we had on our record and the old arrest warrant that stood to indict us. He erased it all—our sins, our stained soul, and our shameful failure to keep his laws—he deleted it all and they cannot be retrieved!

Do you feel something lacking today or feel that He is distant? Take a moment to set your heart on Him. Explore in writing what it feels like to know you are His delight.

_____

_____

_____

_____

_____

_____

_____

_____

_____

_____

_____

_____

_____

_____

_____

_____

_____

_____

"I know your future."

Let Me tell you about your future. It is nothing like your past. I have shaped you with My hands and prepared you for all that is coming. Set your eyes on Me and I will never disappoint you, and you will not be taken captive by the fear of this age. For I am the God of the heavens and I see all that is coming, and I know that you will be held fast by My hand.

Difficulties will come, but so will a greater outpouring. The days will grow darker for those who know not My grace and My power, but for you, My chosen one, you will carry My glory and reveal your Father in heaven. The earth will quake and be broken by the sound of My voice, but your heart will remain at peace, for My covenant of love can never be broken. Sit in My glory until you see as I see. Understanding will fill your heart, and the hope within you will expand and overwhelm any fear. I know what is ahead for you—days of light and glory, years of delight and praise. Never, never give in to the despair around you, but fill your heart with revelation light.

Rest in the realm of peace, and you will know when I

speak and when I move. Don't be afraid of being alone or going forward while others around you sink back. I have called you through the narrow gate to follow Me. I will be enough for you. Even as I sustained My servant Abraham on his journey, I will sustain you and shower you with My love.

Promises long forgotten will now be fulfilled. I have never forgotten any promise I have made to you, so rest in the understanding that I am enough and that I know your future and have marked out every step, bringing you closer to Me and deeper into My glory, until finally, you will awake with My likeness.

PSALM 17:15

As for me, because I am innocent I will see your face
  until I see you for who you really are.
  Then I will awaken with your form and be fully satisfied,
  fulfilled in the revelation of your glory in me!

He has called you to rest in the realm of peace while He handles your future. In what areas of your life do you need to rest more today? Reflect on those and thank Him that He has already marked out every step for you.

_____

_____

_____

_____

_____

_____

_____

_____

_____

_____

_____

_____

_____

_____

_____

"I am your faithful God."

I am your faithful God, unchanging when everything around you changes. My faithfulness is for you to lean upon and believe in. You will learn that there is no hidden shadow or darkness in Me, and there is nothing that will disappoint those who trust in Me. My promises are as true as My Name. I am the God of faithfulness and will always keep My word. All may change around you, but I am unchanging in My faithful love toward you.

Abraham trusted My promises even though he was childless. By the power of My Word, the promise was fulfilled. Isaac trusted My promise and inherited the life and power of eternity. Jacob leaned upon Me when there was nothing else to sustain him. I am the God of Abraham, Isaac, and Jacob—My words are true. What I have promised you, I will fulfill. The words I have spoken over you will all come to pass, for My unending love for you moves My heart to show you My faithfulness.

What I have done for David I will do for you. David believed in My mercy. As He hid behind My wraparound presence, I became His shield. Nothing could harm him as he went out to battle, and nothing will harm you as you stand inside My grace. Never fear, My child, for I am for you and no one can prevail against you.

Nothing can disturb My unshakable faithfulness. When everything crumbles, I remain faithful. When all else fails, the hope of My promise will keep you and guard you. What more could I give to you that I have not already provided? My peace will flow like a river into your troubled heart until you can say, "It is well with my soul."

JAMES 1:17–18

Our generous God freely gives us every good and perfect gift. These wonderful gifts come down to us from the Father of lights, the unchanging God who shines from the heavens with no hidden shadow or hint of darkness. God was delighted to give us new birth by the truth of his infallible Word so that we would fulfill his chosen destiny for us and become the favorite ones of all he created.

His promises are true. Has He not always been
faithful to you? Remember the ways He has proven
faithful in the past. List some of those and allow
your faith to grow as you think on them.

_____

_____

_____

_____

_____

_____

_____

_____

_____

_____

_____

_____

_____

_____

_____

_____

_____

"I will take you deeper."

A deeper place in Me is calling out to a deeper love in you. I will bring you beyond the shallow and superficial and take you deeper into My endless love. The walls that surround you will crumble and fall down to the victory of My love. When everything else fails you, My love will win the day!

This deeper place is filled with love. Your eyes will open and you will see your troubles much differently, for your difficulties are invitations to a greater love. When you have reached the end of your hoarded resources, My love will bring you miracles. Love will open your heart to others, and you will see them as opportunities to demonstrate a greater love. Come deeper into My victorious love that overcomes all things.

I release to you a deeper, more powerful love. You will be wrapped in My presence when you embrace My love. Others may not understand the path of greater love, but I am with you. Others will see this love as weakness, but love will become a virtue burning bright within your soul. Love never fails. Come deeper into My never-failing love, and you will discover the path of true holiness.

2 TIMOTHY 1:6–8

I'm writing to remind you to fan into a flame and rekindle the fire of the spiritual gift God imparted to you when I laid my hands upon you. For God will never give you the spirit of cowardly fear, but the Holy Spirit who gives you mighty power, love, and sound judgment! So never be ashamed of the testimony of our Lord, nor be embarrassed over my imprisonment, but overcome every evil by the revelation of the power of God!

In what areas of your life do you want the Lord
to take you deeper in His love? Declare His mighty
power, love, and sound judgment in each area.

_____

_____

_____

_____

_____

_____

_____

_____

_____

_____

_____

_____

_____

_____

_____

_____

_____

_____

"I give you peace."

Many are restless in this hour. They long for lasting change. They are puzzled over what seems like delay in their advancement. Restlessness comes when you take your eyes off of Me. I call you to rest in My peace and watch Me work. I will be your Sabbath rest.

The distractions are many for My chosen ones. Many voices and many activities can confuse your heart, but in Me there is a peace that transcends all understanding. I give to you, not logic, but peace. My peace can never be disturbed and robbed from you. The peace of your world comes and goes and is easily troubled. Come into My ocean of peace, and I will speak to you the words you need to hear for what is about to come.

You no longer have a place in the world. Your place is with Me. Step into Me, and I will give the place destined for you. My mansions filled with peace and glory await your entrance. There are many resting places in Me. I long to be your undisturbed peace in a time of trouble and rapid change. Come closer to Me and I will come closer to you.

The plans I have for you require that you focus on Me and not on your shifting circumstances.

Confine yourself to Me, as a prisoner of love, and you will be nourished by the eternal.

PSALM 27:4–6

Here's the one thing I crave from God,
  the one thing I seek above all else:
  I want the privilege of living with him every moment in his house,
  finding the sweet loveliness of his face,
  filled with awe, delighting in his glory and grace.
  I want to live my life so close to him
  that he takes pleasure in my every prayer.
In his shelter in the day of trouble, that's where you'll find me,
  for he hides me there in his holiness.
  He has smuggled me into his secret place
  where I'm kept safe and secure—
  out of reach from all my enemies.

What is causing unrest in your life right now—taking you away from His peace that transcends all human understanding? What word is God speaking to you to bring peace to these areas of unrest?

_____

_____

_____

_____

_____

_____

_____

_____

_____

_____

_____

_____

_____

_____

_____

_____

_____

_____

"Be free!"

I am the One who has set you free. Be free to walk in the higher place before My throne. Be free to live in My Spirit Wind as My fruit-bearing child. Everything that could hold you back is now broken from off your life. Be free, child, be free!

I have opened the door of freedom before you. Go forth into the glorious wonder of your future. The freedom I give you is to experience My presence and My power. You are no longer just a servant to a master, but a child of the exalted God. Taste the freedom of My Spirit, and you will never turn back again to that which is dead and barren. The lies that have held you down will be seen for what they are— merely the accusations of the enemy. Today you will begin to understand the freedom I have given you to walk with Omnipotence at your side, for I go with you even until the end of all the ages.

This freedom comes by My Spirit and is enjoyed by those who are filled with My Spirit. Receive the fullness from your Father, and you will bring glory to Me. Come and drink deeper of the fullness. Leave your limitations and all that belongs to the old way of thinking behind you. Drink, drink, drink. My Spirit is the Spirit of love and liberty. As you come out of the shadows and into My life, you will know the truth, and this truth embraced will set you free!

GALATIANS 5:1

Let me be clear, the Anointed One has set us free—not partially, but completely and wonderfully free! We must always cherish this truth and stubbornly refuse to go back into the bondage of our past!

What does it mean to you to be completely free in Him?
How can you walk in that freedom today?
Explore what it looks like to live in this fullness.

_____

_____

_____

_____

_____

_____

_____

_____

_____

_____

_____

_____

_____

_____

_____

_____

_____

_____

_____

"Learn of the way eternal."

I long for you to know Me and to embrace My ways. Come and learn of the way eternal. For the paths of your God will lead you into more joy until it overflows. If you receive My love, even in your difficulty you will know the secret of the wonder of eternity. Don't let appearances deceive you—My love will win every struggle that you face. Even this day I have prepared a hiding place of mercy for you.

Become a disciple, a learner of My ways. There is yet much you have to learn of how I bring you into the highest realm, the place where love prevails. The happiness of life is not found in circumstances. It is discovered when you know that My hand of love is guiding you and leading you even in life's darkest valleys.

Many have had their joy taken from them, for the past is a robber that will come into your thoughts to disturb your joy. The future frightens many, for they have not known My heart of love. Setting your heart on the future may steal away the joy of today. This is the day that I have made for you that you would be glad and experience My love in all things.

There is a stability that will keep you strong and focused, and it comes from knowing the triumph of love in every moment of your life. Set your heart on Me, rely on My victorious grace, and you will be an overcomer that rises into the highest realms. Then you will know Me, not from hearsay, but from heart-deep experiences of intimacy with your God. Come to Me and learn of the way eternal.

PSALM 139:23–24

God, I invite your searching gaze into my heart.
  Examine me through and through;
  find out everything that may be hidden within me.
  Put me to the test, and sift through all my anxious cares.
See if there is any path of pain I'm walking on,
  and lead me back to your glorious, everlasting ways—
  the path that brings me back to you.

Write a prayer inviting God to show you
His eternal ways this day. Ask Him to search you
and show you His loving ways.

_____

_____

_____

_____

_____

_____

_____

_____

_____

_____

_____

_____

_____

_____

_____

_____

"My mercy never ends."

You will never find the end of My love. It stretches wider than the horizon, longer than all eternity, higher than heaven itself, and deeper than the ocean's depths. Many times I have placed you under the fountain of mercy and washed your soul, your conscience, your heart. I restored you because I love you. You will never find the end of My mercy.

I am the God of all grace, and I comfort My people in My love. There are many things around you, even this day, that can distract you and embitter you. But I say, come again to My mercy fountain and be refreshed. The highest mountain peak you can see in all its beauty is still not as high and beautiful as My mercy. Steadfast, unmovable, always giving comfort to My people.

You call Me "Father." And a Father I am to you. I will be there when others fail and when the sky is grey with clouds of despair. No one has yet to exhaust My grace. Over and over I will restore you and forgive you. As far as from the sunrise to the sunset, that's how far I have removed your sins from you. I will give you mercy until the end of time. You will never find the end of My love. Give freely what you have received.

The Redeemer has come to restore all things. And the first sign of restoration is when your eyes open to see Me high and lifted up, with My glorious robe filling you, My temple. Be filled with the glory of My love and receive the fresh infilling from My fountain of mercy, and you will be prepared for what is to come.

PSALM 103:8–10

You're so kind and tenderhearted to those who don't deserve it,
  and so very patient with people who fail you!
  Your love is like a flooding river
  overflowing its banks with kindness.
You don't look at us only to find our faults,
  just so that you can hold a grudge against us.
You may discipline us for our many sins,
  but never as much as we really deserve.
  Nor do you get even with us for what we've done.

What is He washing away from you today with His refreshing fountain of mercy? Write what He is showing you He'd like to cleanse and restore.

_____

_____

_____

_____

_____

_____

_____

_____

_____

_____

_____

_____

_____

_____

_____

_____

_____

_____

"Walk with Me in greater faith."

Many see the horizon filled with clouds and see only a coming storm, but your faith will see the clouds of glory. Did not Ezekiel see the clouds, yet within the storm was the Man of Fire surrounded with lightning and glory? What do you see in the storm?

A soaring faith will bring you into My ways. A sagging faith will bring you down into the ways of men—seeing only what man sees and believing only what man believes. My word is greater, My strength is stronger, and My purpose is more glorious than anything found on earth. Never let your faith be set on the words of men, but on the living words of God! As your eyes focus to the new reality, you will see that I am at work in the storm.

Your faith must never waver, for My word is forever settled in heaven and will not change. Not even if every star fell from the sky and every mountain crumbled into the sea; My covenant of love and My steadfast Word will not be shaken. I am not the author of fear. I am not the God of doubt, but the God of yes and amen! Confusion is nothing more than the dust of the earth blown into the wind by the work of your enemy. Faith is light that creates and empowers and sustains and heals.

Ask for more faith, seek a courageous heart, and knock on My eternal doors, and they will open to you. Watch the miracles come forth from your proclamations of faith and victory! Nothing will turn you aside when you walk with Me by faith, seeing the invisible, loving the eternal, and living for the supernatural. Rise up, mighty one, and take your place with my overcomers. I am with you, and that will always be enough.

HEBREWS 10:22

We come closer to God and approach him with an open heart, fully convinced by faith that nothing will keep us at a distance from him. For our hearts have been sprinkled with blood to remove impurity and we have been freed from an accusing conscience and now we are clean, unstained, and presentable to God inside and out!

What do you see in the storm? God is not the author
of fear and doubt. Meditate on how you see Him
at work in the storm, and describe what you see.

_____

_____

_____

_____

_____

_____

_____

_____

_____

_____

_____

_____

_____

_____

_____

_____

_____

_____